MIRANDA LEARNS THE ART OF NOT FITTING IN

"Morning, second graders. I want to introduce you to Miranda. She's new to Sunnyside," Mr. B said.

Miranda nervously took her seat.
She moved to Sunnyside a month ago and
was sad she had to move and leave her friends.
Miranda had made many friends when she was in first grade,
but was now worried about meeting new friends and fitting in.

The bell rang, and it was time to eat lunch. Miranda looked around the lunchroom and saw a group of girls sitting in the corner. She instantly felt nervous, but she approached them and asked, "Can I sit with you?"

The girls looked at Miranda and said, "Yeah, sure." Miranda sat in silence as the girls talked about their hair, clothes, and who they didn't like in school.

Miranda was glad she didn't have to sit alone in the lunchroom, but she didn't feel like the group of girls cared to talk to her. Miranda felt sad and just wanted to make friends.

When she got home, she told her mom about her first day of school. She wasn't sure if the girls wanted to be her friend.

When Miranda thought about the girls,
she didn't like how they talked meanly about other people.
Miranda didn't like to talk badly about other people.

"I'm going to find a new group of people to hang out with," she told her mom.

The next day at school wasn't any better. At recess, Miranda went over to a group of kids playing kickball.

She didn't like kickball, but wanted to fit in, so she played anyway.

Miranda was picked last to be on a team and even had the ball kicked at her head during the game. All the kids burst into laughter.

At lunch time, Miranda sat alone.
She didn't bother to sit with anyone,
as she felt everyone would ignore her anyway.
The kids also seemed too busy to talk to her. She felt lonely.

After school that day,
Miranda told her mom about her bad day again.
"I just don't fit in," she said.

"Why do you need to fit in?" Miranda's mom asked. This made Miranda think. She was trying to fit in with people she felt were mean and trying to do activities she didn't enjoy.

"Maybe I need to figure out where I want to fit in," Miranda replied. Miranda's mom told her to always relax and pay attention to how she feels when she is trying to make decisions.

Miranda laid in bed, closed her eyes, and took a deep breath. She thought about what made her happy.

The first thing that came to her mind was singing in choir. Miranda remembered how much she loved to sing and how she began singing when she was five.

Miranda told her mother she planned to join the choir at her school the following day.

Miranda's first day as a chorister was great!

She met several new friends that also loved to sing, and was able to discover that she had a lot in common with her new friends.

Lisa, one of Miranda's choir friends, asked her if she wanted to hang out after school. Miranda smiled and said, "Yes!"

Later when she got home that day,
Miranda told her mom about choir and all her new friends.
Miranda realized that by figuring out what made her happy,
she made friends

THE END

Printed in Great Britain
by Amazon